You Are Never
Too Busy

You Are Never
Too Busy

Seeing Your Time
the Way God
Sees It

CONOR GALLAGHER

TAN Books
Gastonia, North Carolina

You Are Never Too Busy: Seeing Your Time the Way God Sees It
© 2023 Conor Gallagher

Unless otherwise noted, Scripture quotations are from the Douay-Rheims Bible.

Cover & interior design and typesetting by www.davidferrisdesign.com

Library of Congress Control Number: 2022951446
ISBN: 978-1-5051-3044-7
Kindle ISBN: 978-1-5051-3045-4
ePUB ISBN: 978-1-5051-3046-1

Published in the United States by
TAN Books
PO Box 269
Gastonia, NC 28053

www.TANBooks.com

Printed in India

"And rising up, he rebuked the wind, and said to the sea: Peace, be still. And the wind ceased: and there was a great calm."

–*Mark 4:39*

"God has created me to do Him some definite service. He has committed some work to me which He has not committed to another. I have my mission. I may never know it in this life, but I shall be told it in the next."

–*Saint John Henry Cardinal Newman*

To those who are a little embarrassed
about being busy

Dear Reader,

I, your unworthy author, must regularly emphasize two points in my spiritual writings: the first is regarding the writing style, and the second is a vital disclaimer.

Regarding style, I have adopted a rather antiquated style of writing. Spiritual writers of old spoke directly to the reader with phrases like "Christian Reader" or "Immortal Soul" or even "Unworthy Christian." Modern sensitives emphasize the first-person plural pronouns of "we" and "us" in an unnecessary attempt to avoid the appearance of paternalism or arrogance. So, when I address "you," as the reader, I am truly saying "we," for the message of this work is intended for myself as much as anyone.

Additionally, my favorite works of spirituality have a very particular voice. It is a voice that calls the reader to conversion, as if the author has but one page, one paragraph, one single sentence to convert the reader to Jesus Christ. Such a voice is starkly different from an intellectual work intended to convince the reader's mind of a superior argument. Here, I hope to jar your soul to conversion with the power and beauty of truth, for your soul and those within your care will be in heaven or in hell ten trillion years from now. We all need a little jarring.

Now, a vital disclaimer: I beg you, remember that preaching and doing are two different things. In fact, I find that I gravitate towards projects in which I need the most improvement.

Sincerely,

Conor Gallagher

PRAYER FOR THOSE WHO ARE BUSY

Heavenly Father,

I know You are here. I know You can hear me and see me. You know my every thought and emotion, my dreams and fears. You govern everything in my life. You experience eternity between every second of my earthly life.

In Your infinite wisdom, You have decided precisely how much time to give me in every situation, with every person I meet, with every suffering I endure. You are the master of my clock, O Lord. And You have planned since before I was born exactly when my lifetime will run out.

In Your infinite love, You have given me no less time than I need to become a holy saint. You have never asked more of me than I can give. You have granted me all the time I need to do Your will.

Most importantly, Father, You have given me the free will to fill every second with surrender to Your will. You have given me the ability to sift through the chaos, the sufferings, and the sins of others and to accept Your holy will amidst it all. You have, indeed, made me resistant to all the worldly attacks on my soul if I simply and only seek Your will every moment of my life.

Throughout these pages, enlighten my mind. Help me to see how much time I waste. Help me to see how many seconds a day I seek my own comforts, my own glory. Help me to see my time the way You see my time. Help me to see my time the way I will see it from the other side of eternity.

Grant me the wisdom to see time only for what it is: Your gift to me that I must never squander. Never a single moment. Never a single second.

Amen.

CONTENTS

The Lord will

free you from

busyness

INTRODUCTION

Have you wondered how the saints were able to accomplish so much with so little time? How Saint John Vianney was able to hear confessions for hours and still find time for his own prayer life? How Pope Saint John Paul II could visit so many countries, write so many encyclicals, and still shepherd the entire Church?

And how about Saint Teresa of Calcutta? Bring your imagination to bear. Picture Mother Teresa, a seventy-year-old religious sister with a hunched back and aching knees, serving the sick and poor in the scorching heat of India. She answers letters until 11:00 p.m., only to rise at 4:30 a.m. the following morning. She attends Mass and makes a Eucharistic holy hour before beginning manual labor by 8:00 a.m., feeding and bathing grown adults who are too sick to do it themselves. She herself eats virtually nothing. Above all, she performs these tasks with a smile on her face—a smile that she chooses out of love, even if she doesn't feel like it.

Throughout her day, Saint Teresa of Calcutta is constantly interrupted. While changing a grown man's diaper, her religious sister asks her whether they should pay the electric bill or buy food. A repair man then asks whether she wants to just patch the roof or replace the entire section. Then a doctor informs her that the small child in her facility needs a leg amputation because the gangrene has gone above the knee. As the bookkeeper whispers that they can't pay for both the roof and the amputation, an AIDs victim vomits on her. And she must at once bathe and change into another sari while the bookkeeper, the repair man, and the doctor are all waiting on her.

This goes on, dear Christian reader, from before sunup to after sundown. And this occurs decade after decade. You might see this sequence as chaotic. But it was not. It was perfect. Mother Teresa was not busy. She was, at each moment, trying to do the will of God. Franticness might have been felt by the bookkeeper, by the repair man, or by the doctor, but not by Mother. She was not busy.

And neither must you be busy.

"MY YOKE IS SWEET"
"Come to me, all you that labour, and are burdened, and I will refresh you. Take up my yoke upon you, and learn of me, because I am meek, and humble of heart: and you shall find rest to your souls. For my yoke is sweet and my burden light" (Matt. 11:28–30).

Herein lies the secret to never being busy again: you always have the perfect amount of time to do the will of God. Nothing else matters. "Too many things to do" no longer matters. Failure, in fact, no longer matters. Fully appreciating this insight gives you tremendous peace, no matter the chaos in your life.

"I do not pray for success, I ask for faithfulness."

Saint Teresa
of Calcutta

At this moment, God wants to bestow one of His greatest gifts on you. He wants to give you the freedom to live like a saint—that is, to do exactly what you are supposed to do in the exact amount of time He gives you to do it. This freedom comes without anxiety or stress because you now have all the time you need to fulfill your duties. Remind yourself of this constantly. You will begin to feel God's peace in only a few moments.

BRAGGING ABOUT BEING BUSY IS A THING OF THE PAST

Being busy might not be what you think it is. It really means that you are, in a manner of speaking, lost or out of control. It means the world has more power over you than God does. It means others have enslaved you. It might mean that you aren't minding your own business. You might not want to tell everyone from here on just how "busy" you are. It is not a point worth bragging about. It is, in fact, the opposite. We will see why shortly.

With God's grace, you are about to see precisely why you should never be busy again. This does not mean you will never have a lengthy to-do list. This does not mean you will never have to move fast or overcome logistical obstacles with family and friends.

But it does mean that you will never think you are too busy to do what really matters. It means that the things that don't get done will be as much of a blessing (maybe more so) as the things you do get done. It means that you will learn how to "meet triumph and disaster, and treat these two imposters just the same," as Rudyard Kipling says in his poem "If." Your failures, dear Christian soul, may well be God's will. And thus, you will never be too busy to do God's will. Or as Saint Teresa of Calcutta would often say, "I do not pray for success, I ask for faithfulness."

IMAGINE THE PERSON YOU WILL BECOME

Christian soul, imagine the kind of friend you will be, the kind of spouse, the kind of parent, the kind of stranger others will meet on the street. Look around. Many people's faces, body language, and tone of voice reflect their busyness. Frankly, the sin of pride makes every person feel busy—or better yet, important. Most of us believe our time is spent wisely. Humble reflection, however, shows otherwise.

> "Be who God meant you to be and you will set the world on fire."
>
> Saint Catherine of Siena

When you learn that you are not too busy, you encounter each circumstance in a different way than most people. You will consider whether this particular moment is in accordance with God's will. So long as it is, you will be perfectly attentive and present. But when the moment is no longer so, you will graciously depart with little or no concern about what other people think about your departure. It is one of the most freeing experiences in life.

Equally as important, you will become a radically different person to those with whom God wants you to associate. Your attention will be almost superhuman because you are not distracted with other "busy stuff" in your life. You will not feel torn because your mind and body will not be in different places. You will be fully present. You will be a better friend, spouse, and parent immediately.

You are about to begin your journey to total freedom of time. Your time belongs to you and God, no one else. His gift to you is to never be busy again.

NEVER TOO BUSY AGAIN

God desires to remove your stress immediately. Why? Because His yoke is sweet, and His burden is light. You may have to run around town and check off a hundred items on your to-do list, but always with His peace in your heart. Yes, God wants to give you His peace every step of the way.

You will never be too busy to be happy. You will never be too busy to succeed or fail for God. You will never be too busy to surrender to Divine Providence. You will never be too busy to be who God is calling you to be and to do what He is asking of you.

WHAT DOES
BUSY MEAN?

You are unimpressed

with being busy

W ords matter. But they can be deceptive. They can literally change meaning over time and can convey different realities depending on the context. So, you should pause for a moment and consider how you use the word *busy*. Often you think to yourself, "I'm too busy," or "We have a busy day ahead of us." To avoid attending a social event, perhaps you give the excuse, "I wish I could, but I am too busy." Or how many times have you been conversing after Mass and someone says, "So, how have you been?" and you almost reflexively answer, "Busy!"—as if that is a unique response.

In fact, the next time someone asks you (out of their own uncertainty of what to really talk about), "Staying busy?" try something that will surprise them: "Not at all. You?" This can lead to an incredible conversation, a conversation that might change the other person's life. In this book, you will find out precisely how to follow up after making such a bold statement.

It only takes a single word by a single person to radically alter the way ideas are shaped. And it only takes a single idea by a single person to radically alter the way we live.

Never use the word *busy* again without meaning it.

Beware: Merriam-Webster lists four definitions of *busy*. Most likely, you might be a little ashamed of the third and fourth definitions. By the end of this little work, I hope you won't be as proud (if you are proud right now) of the first and second.

FIRST DEFINITION: OCCUPIED

Merriam-Webster often gives a short definition along with a synonym to match it. The most basic definition of busy is "engaged in action" or "occupied." When people ask you, "So, you been busy recently?" this is what they mean (they also mean the second definition).

Consider how much of your life is "occupied." When you tell people how busy you are, it is like you are holding up a sign that says "occupied" and thus "you cannot enter." Do you know what else has a sign on it that says "occupied"? A porta-john.

Pride makes you believe that you are important, often more so than others. Pride also convinces you of your productivity, your unique difficulties and crosses, and how much martyrdom you are willing to endure.

A pernicious subtlety is at work here. When you communicate "I am occupied," you are also implying "You are fortunate if I let you in." That's right. Perhaps you feel a little prestigious about being slightly off limits.

> *"I knew nothing. I was nothing. Therefore God picked me out."*
>
> Saint Catherine Laboure

No doubt, you *must* be off limits to most people. In fact, holiness involves saying no more frequently than saying yes to those infringing on your time. The point, rather, is that humility requires you to consider whether being "busy" tickles your ego.

At the same time, *The Rule of Saint Benedict* states that "idleness is the enemy of the soul." But this is different from being occupied for the sake of being occupied. Saint Benedict intended his monks to occupy themselves with holy work and holy prayer with one end in mind: God's glory. Therefore, it is staggering how many of us desire to look "occupied." While you want your busyness to give the impression of importance, what it really does is show that you are not in control of your time and attention.

Are you afraid of your sign saying "vacant"? If you don't give off the air of busy, might people invade? Well, are you competent enough to say "No, thank you. I have a clear focus on my priorities right now"? Instead of using "I'm too busy" as an excuse for saying no to someone, consider saying that you don't want to *become* busy by doing things that are outside of your priorities.

> "Humility, humility, and always humility. Satan fears and trembles before humble souls. The Lord is willing to do great things, but on the condition that we are truly humble."
>
> Saint Padre Pio

Humility requires that you answer the following questions: Are you too much of a high achiever to appear at rest? Does the notion of leisure smack of laziness? If so, you have some spiritual work ahead of you, as we all do. Humility, however, purifies your motives for working hard. Humility will transform your hard work from self-centeredness to selflessness. It will not only open your soul to grace but also repel the demons from your daily activity.

SECOND DEFINITION: BUSTLING

The second definition of busy is "full of activity: bustling." If you are like most, *full of activity* has a nice ring to it. But *bustling*, not so much. *Bustling* is an excellent word for busy. It makes you think of a bustling shopping mall—people moving about frantically. It reminds you of a colony of bees—so efficient, so hard-working, so much unison. But remember, a worker bee lives sixty days and literally dies of exhaustion. Hence a colony of bees is often a better metaphor for communism than Catholicism. There is no room for bustling in the life of an authentic Christian.

"My family is so busy" often means "We are bustling about," often without a clear purpose. Bustling quickly becomes chaos. Reflect upon the last time you were worn out from too much coming and going. How many times does one family have to get in the car every day? How many times must one family buy groceries? How much correspondence is necessary to plan an outing for the kids? How much time do you waste on your smartphone?

Here, let us focus on digital bustling, for we are all guilty of it to varying degrees.

Have you recently been on a group text in which every person replied to the entire group? One single text to ten people can literally result in dozens of dings in your life. One person replies, and another gives a thumbs up, and another "likes" but then "unlikes" and "loves" instead. And on and on and on.

We must all learn to communicate like adults. Stop the bustling through text messaging. This is not just a pet peeve of the sensible but an indication of a spiritual malaise. To pepper other people's lives with needless emojis and dings and little emotional bursts through your fingertips tells the world that you have found little better to do with your time and that you do not mind interrupting others from more important matters in their own lives. It is sophomoric and selfish. It is Chinese water torture to the entire group, even when they think they enjoy it. And the fact that group texting does not have a "reply" option but forces you to "reply all" proves that the creators of your labyrinth strategically plan for you to bustle about the lives of the entire group all day long. On your deathbed, you will not wish you had sent one more text, scrolled for one more second, or shared one more silly meme.

Stepping back from digital bustling, you can see that bustling is all around you. The sneaky part of this trap is that all this bustling seems necessary for a healthy, happy life, right? After all, the majority of this bustling isn't for you! It is for your kids, your spouse, your friends, or your community.

This is a lie.

Your kids, your spouse, your friends, and your community need you, not your busyness. They don't need you involved in too many activities. They don't need your input on everything. They don't need your tweet, post, or text. They need *you*.

You can only become the person God desires you to be if you are free from the worldly distractions around you.

THIRD DEFINITION: MEDDLING

The definition "occupied" was not overly offensive. "Bustling" was a little less pleasant-sounding but still acceptable given that you feel like a busy bee fluttering about to and fro. But "meddling"? No. You most certainly do not want to self-associate with being one who meddles. That is beneath your dignity. Even the most meddlesome people deny being meddlers, just like gossips deny gossiping.

If you are an extremely busy person, however, you must ask yourself whether you are a meddler. The answer is yes. You are. Everyone meddles at times. The question for you is how much do you meddle?

> "As he that takes a dog by the ears, so is he that passes by in anger and meddles with another man's quarrel."
>
> Proverbs 26:17

Meddling is defined as "to interest oneself in what is not one's concern: interfere without right of propriety."

If you had lived a hundred years ago, you would have had more difficulty meddling in other people's business. But now that you always have a smartphone in your pocket, you are in constant contact with too many people. Plus, you can now receive news about people at the speed of light. And now you have the means to express your opinions and feelings about everything. Consequently, meddling is a substantial barrier to your own sanctity.

If you really want to be a saint (rather than a typical phone-addicted, lukewarm Christian), you might consider spending an hour in solitude and assessing all of your phone activity for the last month. Be brutally honest with yourself. How much of your phone time (text, talk, searching, social, etc.) aided your spiritual development? How much time involved complaining about children, spouses, or friends? How much time involved a third party not in the conversation?

If you are brutally honest with yourself, you may find that sometimes you essentially gossip about people under the guise of "getting advice" or "seeking prayers for another." Those with a busy tongue have a bad habit of shrouding sinful talk with pious overtures. As Saint Peter said, "For he that will love life, and see good days, let him refrain his tongue from evil, and his lips that they speak no guile" (1 Ptr. 3:10).

Meddling is at an all-time high. You are not immune to it. But you can most certainly see it for what it is.

"Let your speech be always in grace seasoned with salt: that you may know how you ought to answer every man."

Colossians 4:6

"For where your treasure is,
there will your heart be also."

LUKE 12:34

FOURTH DEFINITION:
FULL OF DISTRACTING DETAILS

You know a "busy" design when you see one. It has too many elements. It is filled with clutter. It lacks the elegance of white space. What does it tell you about the designer? Perhaps he lacks consistency of thought. Perhaps he clings to his little treasures like a dragon clings to gold. Perhaps he is overcompensating for a shortcoming. Maybe you have visited a house that is filled with gaudy trinkets and overly designed furniture and clashing motifs. This, too, says something about the homeowner.

Within minutes of your death, Christian reader, you will see your life like one of these gaudy, over-designed, cluttered rooms. You will see that you and only you filled your life with these worthless trinkets. You will be confronted with your inability to detach from people, places, and things. You will see what little room you left for God and His will for you.

Your busyness comes from distracting detail that is totally and completely unnecessary. In a vacuum, each of these little trinkets in your life is not overly burdensome. But the cumulative fact is that your life is so full that you are distracted. Distracted from what? From God's simple and direct plan for your life.

God whispers. You can't hear Him if you are distracted.

CHAPTER

2

YOUR
SECRET SIN

Once your secret sin

is no longer hidden,

it loses its power

over you

D o you take offense at one claiming to know your secret sin? For it is really no secret at all. Assuming you are like most, your secret sin is that sin which manifests as a secret. It is the same with most of us.

It is a secret because of the way it attacks you. It is a secret because it is like quicksand: it slowly drags you down. In fact, the more you move about, the faster you sink. It is a secret because it hides behind all of your busyness, your hectic schedule, your exhaustion, your coming and going, and your constant credit card purchases. It is secret because it hides behind all "the good things" you are so busy doing. It is a secret because you are too busy to even consider it, which is its primary tactic.

Lust is not much of a secret. When you are lustful, you know it. Gluttony usually (though not always) results in a visible manifestation of obesity or drunkenness. Anger often reveals itself in a nasty facial expression or an explosion of violence. Pride, envy, and greed manifest in arrogance or self-absorption, evident to those close to you.

But the secret sin is much sneakier. The secret sin comes in a way that most people praise. It comes in worldly accolades. It comes in the prize of modernity: productivity.

Your secret sin, dear Christian reader, is sloth.

"God has created me to do Him some definite service. He has committed some work to me which He has not committed to another. I have my mission. I may never know it in this life, but I shall be told it in the next."

Saint John Henry Newman

THE MYTH OF PRODUCTIVITY

The father of lies, Satan, tempted our first mother with the beguiling notion of progress. He told her that if she ate of the fruit, her eyes would be opened and she would be as a god (see Gen. 3:5). Eve was tempted by progress. She believed that there was something more to be had than God had already given her—for apparently "dominion over the fishes of the sea, and the fowls of the air, and the beasts, and the whole earth, and every creeping creature that moveth upon the earth" (Gen. 1:16) was not enough. No, she wanted to have more, to perceive more, to be more than God intended for her.

Yes, the father of lies tempted our first parents with the notion of progress, and he continues to do so with you today.

Today, the fruits we desire are automation, speed, ease, and excessive access to everything. Enormous amounts of productivity had to occur for you to be able to consume everything you consume in rapid fashion. You pay big bucks for these modern perks. You can figure the expense by checking your bank statement. But what is it really costing you and your loved ones?

The evil one promises you a life of luxury if you would but taste his favorite fruit— the fruit of progress, the fruit of productivity. Satan's mastery of technology has slowly taken away our dominion over the

> *"Get more done!"*
>
> Satan

earth and given technology dominion over us. We have become hamsters on the wheel of progress, cogs in the wheel of automation, and, worse, victims of spiritual genocide. Frankly, saints usually want to be left alone.

Automation is putting our humanity at stake, for the very things that make us human cannot be automated. Discussion between

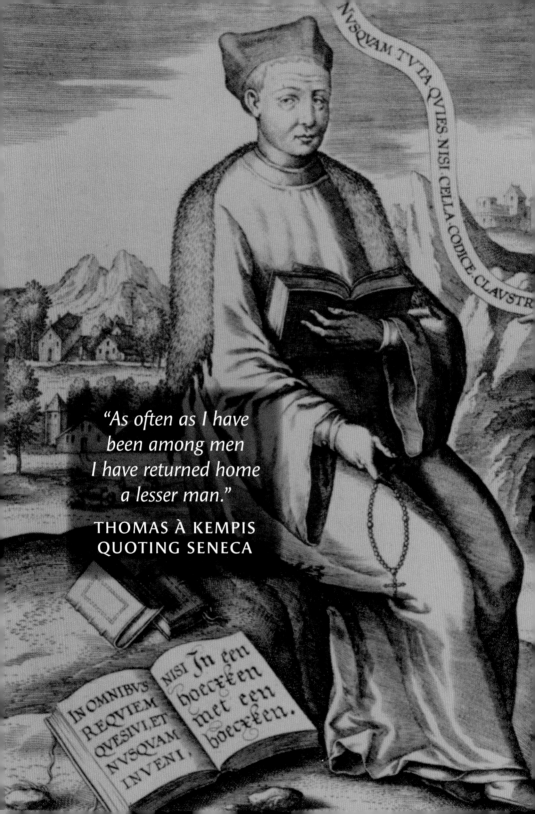

"As often as I have been among men I have returned home a lesser man."

THOMAS À KEMPIS
QUOTING SENECA

friends is being replaced by posts between "followers." "Smart" phones remind us of those things worth remembering, such as our friends' phone numbers and family members' birthdays. The internet has ruined the rich experience of taking little children to the library. Television and Netflix have replaced family discussions in the evening.

We are losing our humanity by the digital minute.

THE SIN OF SLOTH

Throughout the centuries, the evil one has had his weapons of choice. He does not wield just any tool to destroy souls. No, like a master craftsman, he picks his instrument carefully and precisely. At first glance, it may appear that his weapon for the modern age is lust. But no. The sin of our age, our age of busyness, is sloth.

Progress keeps the modern man so busy, so focused on improvement, so obsessed with productivity. Progress keeps modern parents so intent on raising perfect students, and athletes, and musicians, and . . . and . . . and! In the end, there is little room for joy, for worship, for humble submission to God's will.

This brings us to the definition of sloth.

The Angelic Doctor, Saint Thomas Aquinas, defines sloth as "sorrow for spiritual goods" and "sluggishness of the mind which neglects to begin good."[1] It is your obsession for things beyond your reach, just as Eve desired in the Garden, that drains your desire for God—or even leads us to desire humanity for ourselves. Yes, you seek to become more and more conformed to the world rather than conformed to the will of God. You chase after the glory of man rather than the glory of God by wasting your life on things that hold no eternal significance.

1. *Summa Theologiae* II-II, Q. 35, Art. 1.

As a result, sloth slowly drains your spiritual energy. It is the sin that makes you sleep in rather than awaken early for Morning Prayer. It is the sin that makes you more dependent on a morning coffee than on a morning offering. It is the sin that makes you reticent in speaking on spiritual matters with your family and friends. It is the sin that makes you more "conservative" than Christian. It is the sin that makes you groan when it is time to get the kids ready for Mass. It is the sin that leads you to

> *"Sloth is a sorrow for spiritual goods."*
>
> Saint Thomas Aquinas

deliberate distractions during Mass, especially people-watching. It is the sin that makes you impatient for Mass to end. And at the end of a long day, it is the sin that leads to watching a movie rather than reading a spiritual book. This is sloth.

Ask yourself, do you have energy to check your smartphone every sixteen minutes but not enough bandwidth to pray a Rosary with your family for sixteen minutes? Check your phone. How many times do you send a text message each day? The average person under the age of forty-five sends more than eighty-five texts per day.

Imagine if you said eighty-five Hail Marys per day.

And you are too busy?

THE DEVIL'S TROJAN HORSE

The devil's stratagem calls to mind the Trojan horse that was wheeled into the city of Troy as a magnificent gift. Under the cover of night, the bloodthirsty Greek warriors descended from the belly of the horse and slaughtered the Trojans in wicked and ruthless and even sacrilegious fashion.

Lucifer's Trojan horse for the modern world is progress, efficiency, and productivity. "Get more and more done, faster and faster." As a master strategist, the devil puts into motion the famous words of Sun Tzu, the sixth-century Chinese military general, "All warfare is based on deception. Hence, when we are able to attack, we must seem unable; when using our forces, we must appear inactive."

Most people envision a slothful man as a couch potato who stuffs his mouth with chips and beer. But the devil is more deceptive than that. The slothful man is, rather, one who wears himself out with work, fitness, social activities, consumption of news, and downloading the newest productivity app.

And sloth is not just committed by men. The strung-out mother is guilty of sloth when she feels she must respond to a text at red lights or while the little ones are asking questions, when she must register the kids for this activity and that one, when she feels she must work out to keep her figure and must get her hair and nails done just to keep her sanity, when she feels that another baby would ruin everything, or when the little voice at knee level, trying to tug on the yoga pants while saying, "Mommy, mommy, mommy," is no longer a sweet sound to the mother's ear but an annoyance—an interruption to her.

> "All warfare is based on deception. Hence, when we are able to attack, we must seem unable; when using our forces, we must appear inactive."
>
> Sun Tzu

Dear mother, understand that it is a choice. You choose where your attention goes. Of course there is too much to do in twenty-four hours. You have too much on your plate. But in the next few minutes, you will be confronted with a choice of exactly how to

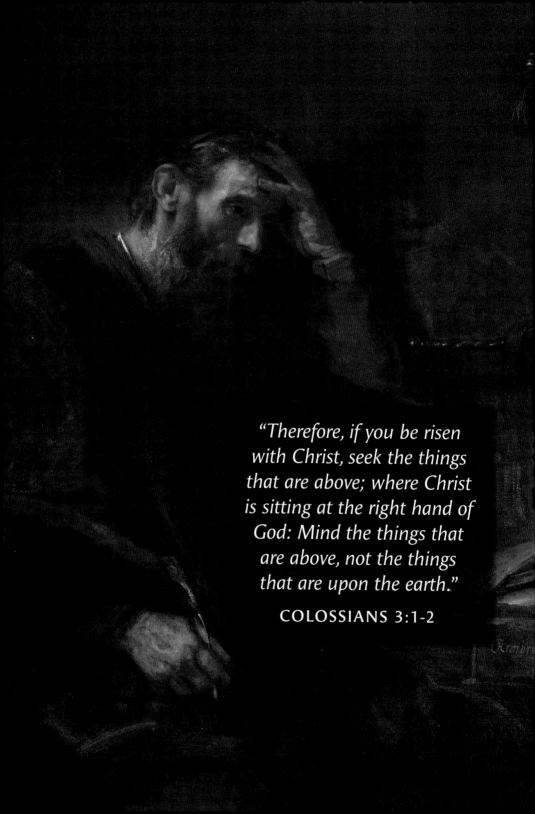

"Therefore, if you be risen with Christ, seek the things that are above; where Christ is sitting at the right hand of God: Mind the things that are above, not the things that are upon the earth."

COLOSSIANS 3:1-2

spend your time, whether that is reading this book, checking your email, or speaking to your kids. No one can make the decision for you. It is your choice. Whatever that choice may be, know that you have never been nor ever will be too busy to do God's will in a particular moment.

Dear Christian, look around at so many well-intentioned people (particularly parents). See that everyone is exhausted with needless activity. How is it that we live in a world of nearly magical automation *and yet* are more exhausted than previous generations who labored manually? We are exhausted because nature and grace are the nourishment for our humanity. And we are malnourished. We are filling our spiritual bellies with the addictive and artificial sweetness of productivity and efficiency, but we are lacking the life-giving nutrients of silence, stillness, prayer, friendship, beauty, and leisure.

Again, are you sure you are "too busy"? Maybe now you see that being "busy" is exactly what the devil wants. Remember this the next time someone asks you, "So, you stayin' busy?"

ALL THE TIME YOU NEED

Freedom to do

what you are

supposed to do

No matter what madness is going on around you, you should ponder a life-changing truth: you are never too busy to do the will of God. Period. It is, dear reader, impossible to be too busy to do the will of God.

Why? Because no matter how chaotic your life is, you have the freedom to choose God's will in whatever happens in that moment, which might entail ending the madness. Perhaps you have foolishly overcommitted yourself and are now stuck finishing what you began. It may not be God's will to walk away. It may be God's will to persevere, but with a humble surrender to His will in doing so.

Begin by surrendering everything. Do nothing without considering the will of God. This is a living prayer, a prayer that can be said continually in every situation.

And this disposition of always seeking the will of God will allow you to avoid overcommitting to people and activities. You will begin to find comfort in having more time with God. You will wonder how you ever found time for everything else.

NEVER WASTE YOUR DUTIES

When you are doing the routine, the mundane, the stuff that feels "busy," you must learn to offer it to your heavenly Father as a sacrifice. His will hides within each of the duties of your state in life. As soon as you approach the altar of sacrifice, whether it be a boardroom table or a kitchen table, you are offering up your duties. You are never too busy to make this sacrifice. If you are conscious, you can do it. In fact, you can even sacrifice those moments that you are unconscious. How? Offer up your sleep before you retire for the night.

> *"Pray without ceasing."*
>
> 1 Thessalonians 5:17

You are never too busy to offer up all that you have, all that you are doing. Your external actions may not change immediately. You might still be dragged around town and burdened with endless communication, but you can say to Our Lord, "Thy will be done." You can say, "If this is not Your will, please take it away from me." You can say, "I'm sorry I put myself here, Lord, but I offer up my stupidity to You and beg for Your grace the next time I have a decision to make."

You are never too busy to do God's will because His will underlies all your actions. Do not fool yourself into thinking doing God's will always means doing particular things. Rather, doing God's will means doing particular things in a particular way. It is found in the disposition of your heart at every single moment.

Life is not about counting the number of tasks to be done or goals to be realized, but the intensity of your surrender to Divine Providence.

OTHERS CANNOT MAKE YOU TOO BUSY

So far, we have only considered how your own decisions lead to busyness. You may be saying to yourself, "The craziness and stress comes from others! Not me!" Perhaps you blame your demanding boss who is oblivious to your full workload. Perhaps you blame your children who can't do their chores right, or your self-absorbed teenagers who think they are overworked. Perhaps you blame annoying or weird people who email and text stupid questions or complicate the simplest of situations.

How many hours of your day are filled by the imperfections, idiosyncrasies, and sins of others? In fact, when you are left to

"Don't say, 'that person bothers me.' Think, 'That person sanctifies me.'"

Saint Josemaría Escrivá

your own devices, things go much smoother. Thus, you can easily conclude that you are busy because everyone else is intrusive and difficult.

Do you realize, Christian reader, that the great saints dealt with the same types of people? Do you realize that God takes these people into consideration as He judges your sanctity? Imagine how silly it would be for Him to say, "Well, Jane can't be holy because the people around her are obnoxious. Sorry, Jane! Heaven isn't for you!" On the contrary, these trying circumstances are Almighty God's way of helping you become a saint. Truly, difficult people are a gift, but we can only see this with supernatural faith. Admittedly, this is one of the most challenging teachings of the saints and spiritual masters.

When you, Christian soul, are exhausted and frustrated at everyone else letting you down, you must do the following. First, you must humbly recognize how you have let God down. If you are as competent as you think, then God has extremely high expectations of you! In other words, the more frustrated you are with the failings of others, the more God will be frustrated with your failings. Does this mean you never correct your

"And unto whomsoever much is given, of him much shall be required."

Luke 12:48

little ones when they fail to clean their room? No. Does it mean you let employees be lazy? No. God wants you to take decisive action. But He never wants you to lose peace and happiness for doing what He wants you to do. The obnoxious kid or the weird neighbor who aggravates you to death has absolutely no power over your focus and attention on doing the will of God.

In short, other people cannot make you busy. They can force action upon you. But they can never control how your will is surrendered to God. They can never take your peace and happiness. Only you give that up for the short-lived relief of getting frustrated and blaming others.

You will never get rid of the stress until you understand that you are the only source of that stress.

STRESS IS GONE

How stressed would you be if you knew, without any doubt, that you were doing the will of God?

The fact that you are never too busy to do the will of God is one of the most consoling truths you could ever ask for. Why is this consoling? Because your stress, your anxiety very often comes from feeling that you "don't have enough time" to do everything. Your own expectations are your greatest enemy.

As will be discussed shortly, there are two, and only two, possibilities when you feel that God has given you too much to do. This will be discussed in chapter 5.

Stress is thinking about something when you don't want to. You have so many competing thoughts at one time. You think about work, family, friends, and personal goals, and then you hide from it all by scrolling through a meaningless news feed. When you

"So what are we worried about? God is looking after us and yet we are full of anxiety!"

Saint Claude de la Colombière

find yourself looking at these headlines, consider whether you are trying to avoid reality.

If you are like most people, you are not *per se* against thinking about finances; you just don't want to think about it when you are grocery shopping. You are not *per se* against grocery shopping, but you don't want to think about it when you are dealing with the insurance company. You are not *per se* against dealing with the insurance company, but you don't want to think about it when you are driving to soccer practice.

But notice what is happening to you here: your body is one place, and your mind is elsewhere. The trick of the saints is to see the task before you as the will of God.

Again, how stressed would you be, if you knew with certainty that you were doing God's will?

FREEDOM IN THE MINUTES

With all the time management systems at your disposal, with all the productivity apps downloaded to people's smartphones, you are still overwhelmed. You must begin by confronting these simple questions: What is the purpose of your time? And for whom do you live?

If you are forty-three years old and you live until you are eighty-three, you will have 2,080 Mondays available to you. Those Mondays are made up of 49,920 hours. Those hours are made up of 2,995,200 minutes. Those minutes are made up of 179,712,000 seconds. And that's just Mondays!

Stop and think. Can you possibly conclude that 2,995,200 minutes on Mondays isn't enough time to find peace and happiness in fulfilling God's will? Or will you surrender your Mondays to keeping up with the world, to the demands of your cell phone, or to needless busy work?

Even if a single task was never removed from your life over those next three million minutes, you can still live every one as if each one is ample time to do exactly what God wants you to do.

You, dear busy person, can find freedom in the minutes to take refuge in God's will. Whether you are digging a ditch or changing a diaper, you can peacefully fulfill God's will minute by minute.

You can choose to use the crutch of "I am too busy" or you can find God's will in absolutely everything.

The choice is yours.

PLENTY OF TIME FOR UNCONDITIONAL SURRENDER

The sacrament of the present moment is a very real thing. God is the eternal now. He is not in the past. He is not in the future. He is in the present. The closest we can get to Him in time is in the present moment.

When you feel overwhelmed or frustrated, stop and ask yourself a very specific question: What I am doing right now? The answer must be extraordinarily specific. It is not general.

"Our business is to attain heaven;
everything else is a sheer waste of time."

SAINT VINCENT DE PAUL

Let's say you are about to have a tough conversation with a teenager who has made you angry. Right before he steps into the room, you think about the usual: the conversation starts off normal but becomes heated. Before long, you are yelling and the teenager becomes disrespectful.

Instead, ask yourself, "What I am doing right now?" The answer is something like this: "I am being a parent, and I desire to be a saintly one. I am preparing to talk with my teenager. I am committing to not raising my voice. I am making certain that my teenager leaves our conversation after seeing my authority and affection. I am a loving parent who is about to have a conversation that can go wrong if I lose my cool. I am a loving parent who is about to do God's will to the best of my ability. And I am hoping that my child sees that. If he doesn't, God's will be done."

In that moment, you are not too busy. You have all the time in the world to prepare to be a holy parent because preparation only takes a few seconds.

Imagine an army that unconditionally surrenders. It doesn't take long to wave the white flag. But it takes weeks or months to make a conditional surrender. One must draw up and debate every iota of terms and conditions. You don't have time to partially surrender to God. But you have plenty of time, in the sacrament of the present moment, to surrender unconditionally to Him—over and over and over again.

The truest sacrament of the present moment is the moment of unconditional surrender. There is no better way to spend your time than being perfectly surrendered to God's holy will. Just as those in holy orders and the religious life fulfill God's will through obedience, so God invites all people, from the pope to the mother of ten children, to do His will in peace and happiness.

GOD'S TWO WAYS OF FREEING YOU FROM BUSYNESS

The incredible gift

of never being

too busy again

Call to mind the story of Mother Teresa in the beginning of this book. She had a frantic environment around her, but she was not frantic. She was at peace in each moment. She was not too busy to be faithful. In her case, this also resulted (though not always) in her being wildly successful.

Mother Teresa famously said, "I know God will never give me more than I can handle, I just wish He didn't trust me so much." But what did she really mean by this?

When you feel overwhelmed, whether your day is filled with many silly things or even filled entirely with good things, there are only two options:

1. God wants you to stop doing something; or

2. God wants you to fail at something.

Dear Christian reader, this simple reality should immediately give you an enormous sense of relief. God is either going to take things off your plate (with your help) or He wants you to fail, which is not really a failure!

> "I know God will never give me more than I can handle, I just wish He didn't trust me so much."
>
> Saint Teresa of Calcutta

These two options are mercies that can only come from your heavenly Father. They are glorious. They are worthy of your deepest contemplation. They will radically alter how you perceive time and tasks for the rest of your life. Remember, it is God's will for you to be happy right now, not just in heaven. Even in the midst of chaos and stress, our hearts can rest with Him in peace. And then you will know the peace of the martyrs, the peace of great saints. You will know heaven while still on earth. God wants you to practice being in heaven—right now.

THE FIRST WAY GOD FREES YOU:
STOP DOING SOMETHING

The first way God frees you is by allowing you to stop doing something. Imagine that Jesus Himself descends from the clouds, grabs your day planner, flips to the to-do list, and with His celestial feather pen, strikes an item off your list. He looks at you and says, "There. You are no longer responsible for this. I have freed you. Go in peace."

Your job is to figure out exactly what that item is. You might say to yourself, "Yeah, but that's the hard part! I don't know what to stop doing!" But have you really asked Jesus Christ specifically for the answer? Have you ever taken your to-do list to prayer, invoking the gifts of the Holy Spirit received at Confirmation? You often ask the Lord what you should do. How often do you ask Him what you should *not* do?

You must exercise the virtue of prudence to discern what to stop doing. While prudence is a natural virtue, you should pray to the Holy Spirit to enliven your mind. You can also invoke the gift of wisdom from Confirmation when seeking to delete items off your to-do list. It is astounding how much God gives us clarity when we ask for it.

If you are like most people, you carry so much weight on your shoulders, like a man hiking through the desert with an over-packed backpack, thinking that every item is important. The heavy load will kill him. He will die of thirst if he does not divest himself of mostly everything.

And you, dear Christian sojourner, how important is your journey to the afterlife? Are you carrying more than you are supposed to? Is there something that God wants to take off your to-do list? How could you know the answer to this rudimentary question if you have not *asked* Him!

Most likely, there are many things He wants you to get rid of—
right now. We aren't talking about the stupid stuff. That's obvious.
He fully expects you to use your brain and cast off the silliness.
But there are other good and edifying activities that He wants
to free you from. There are relationships, associations, hobbies,
goals, ambitions, and even charitable activities that God has said,
"Yes, thank you for trying to do these things. But no more. I take
it from you. You are free from it because I want you to focus on
something even greater in your life."

You cannot stumble into this awareness. You must pray your way
into it. Such an awareness only comes from an intimate, personal
relationship with God. Truly, this awareness is a gift from God to
those who are receptive to His grace and want nothing else but
to live a holy life. He will most likely free you from much of what
you believe to be His will.

But what if He doesn't? Would God ever give you more than you
can handle? What a glorious question. The answer follows.

THE SECOND WAY: FAIL

Did God give Saint Paul more than his neck could handle as the
sword came down upon it? Yes. Did God give Saint Lawrence
more heat than he could handle as he baked on the grill to
death? Yes. Did God give Saint Maximillian Kolbe more than he
could handle in the little syringe filled with carbolic acid? Yes.

God often gives us more than our bodies can handle. Never, however, does He give us more than our souls can handle.

These martyrs, in a very real way, failed. They failed to escape
their captors. They failed to convert their captors before their own
deaths. They lasted till death, but they were still bound by the
laws of the physical universe.

> *"I will attempt day by day to break my will into little pieces. I want to do God's Holy Will, not my own."*
>
> Saint Gabriel Possenti

Perhaps you never thought of the martyrs as failures. Of course not. But they in fact failed at many worldly endeavors. Mother Teresa may have failed at many of the things on her to-do list: save this child's leg from gangrene / patch a hole in the roof / prepare my Nobel Peace Prize speech / buy food for the twenty-seven people who arrived at our house yesterday / beg the US ambassador for bread / wash my sari with vomit on it / respond to all my correspondence before bedtime / meet the ten new novices at morning Mass / change diapers for an hour before breakfast / meet the Dalai Lama for breakfast.

How many of these things did Mother fail at? Many. This failure was God's glorious gift to her. She was destined for daily failures. It was her cross. It is the school of Calvary. Failure brings humility. Failure brings wisdom. Failure brings unity with Christ crucified.

Perhaps Our Lord took away some of Mother Teresa's tasks over time. But many of them He did not. He wanted her to die a white martyrdom as opposed to a red martyrdom.

Even though your life might be filled with many good things that overwhelm you, God may be calling you to a white martyrdom. You may not be called to severe fasting or to wear a hair shirt, but you may be called to a life of failure. Perhaps you fail to live up to others' expectations because you rarely complete your work, or your performance is mediocre at best. Imagine that! Imagine being called to a life of worldly mediocrity! A superb martyrdom. Perhaps God has called you to an ordinary life filled with extraordinary love. Very often, the greatest accomplishments are unseen by the world, especially those accomplishments that God cherishes the most.

"Red martyrdom" is due
to torture or violent death
by religious persecution.
"White martyrdom" was
named by St. Jerome for
those who live according
to strict asceticism and
slowly die to self.

If you are worldly, you see certain mediocrity, failure, and disappointment as crosses to be avoided. If you are heavenly, you might see these things as white martyrdom offered in self-denial and sacrifice.

Saint Rose Philippine Duchesne, an early American missionary from France, is the patron saint of perseverance and adversity. She is the saint who failed at everything—in a manner of speaking. Saint Joseph Benedict Labre was another French saint who failed at everything. In fact, he was a wandering homeless man who was turned down by multiple religious orders. And so he spent his life in the streets and churches of Rome, adoring the Holy Eucharist.

"Those who desire only the good pleasure of God abide in peace even in the midst of failure, for God has not told us that He requires success of us."

Saint Rose Philippine Duchesne

What is God calling you to fail at? When you have given something your all, and your prayer confirmed that this was what you were supposed to be doing, the only logical conclusion is that God's holy providence loved your failure. He applauded your failure. The angels and saints looked with admiration upon your failure. They see your failure as the very tool etching your name into the eternal ledger of the elect. And upon your entry into paradise, you will see so many of your successes as failures and so many of your failures as successes.

You are never too busy to fail at those things God wants you to fail at.

You are never too busy.

Living your life

without ever saying

to yourself or others

"I am too busy"

CONCLUSION

Dear Christian soul, words matter. They are the incarnation of the thoughts that occupy your mind. Aristotle defined humans as *zoon logon.* This can be translated as "rational animal" or "speaking animal." For Aristotle, the fact that we can speak made us different from every other animal. Speaking is, in a certain respect, the telltale sign of being imbued with the image and likeness of Almighty God.

And thus, the words you say are vitally important to your well-being. When you verbalize something, you almost give it life. The Son is the *logos* of the Father, the Word.

"In the beginning was the Word, and the Word was with God, and the Word was God."

John 1:1

Words are extremely important to a true Christian. Will you, dear reader, take the word *busy* seriously from now on? Perhaps much of this little book strikes you as semantics. But the author would wager a great deal on the notion that the saints didn't go around telling everyone how "busy" they were. In fact, all the evidence is to the contrary. Over thirty years and with a sense of peace and serenity, Saint Frances Cabrini established over sixty missionary institutions, including hospitals and educational and social services, before her death at the age of sixty-seven. Countless people attest that Pope Saint John Paul II always seemed at ease, at peace, and fully present to whomever he was speaking with. The same was said of Mother Teresa. The same was said of Padre Pio. The same was said of Saint Francis de Sales. And the same can be seen about Jesus in the Gospels.

Judas was busy.

Challenge yourself to stop saying how busy you are. Your thoughts will follow your words. If you stop saying "I'm so busy," you will eventually stop thinking "I'm so busy." This isn't just some silly positive thinking technique. Rather, it is the reality of your human nature—a rational nature, a speaking nature. Metaphorically speaking, your words are made incarnate. Be careful what you say, for you will begin to believe it.

Remember, failing is a perfectly beautiful option. But thinking (even somewhat unconsciously) that you are too busy to do the will of God is beneath you, and way beneath God.

The choice is yours. God desires His saints to be free from busyness. And God is calling you to be a saint. But it begins now. By humbly submitting yourself to Divine Providence, you will be able to embrace this one, simple, freeing truth:

You are never too busy.

THE AUTHOR

Mr. Conor Gallagher earned both his masters in philosophy and juris doctorate from the Catholic University of America. He began his professional career as a law clerk to the Honorable Robert J. Conrad, chief judge of the Western District of North Carolina. He has been an adjunct professor of philosophy, political philosophy, and Catholic social doctrine at Belmont Abbey College.

Mr. Gallagher has served on many boards, including the Board of Visitors for the Columbus School of Law at the Catholic University of America, the Association of Catholic Publishers, and more recently, the Board of Trustees for Holy Angels, a residence for more than eighty disabled individuals.

Currently, Mr. Gallagher serves on the Board of Advisors at Saint Joseph College Seminary, the minor seminary for the Diocese of Charlotte, and the Board of Trustees at Belmont Abbey College. He is also the founder and executive director of the Benedict Leadership Institute at Belmont Abbey College.

Mr. Gallagher is currently the CEO of Good Will Publishers and its subsidiary, TAN Books. He is a regular speaker at parishes, homeschool conferences, Legatus chapters, and is often a guest on numerous radio programs, podcasts, and TV shows. He is the author of *Parenting for Eternity: A Guide to Raising Children in Holy Mother Church* (TAN Books, 2021), *Still Amidst the Storm* (TAN Books, 2018), and *If Aristotle's Kid Had an iPod* (Saint Benedict Press, 2013). Books to be released in the near future include numerous other books in the TAN Direction series you are holding now, plus a meditative book on the life of Christ entitled *The Meekness and Humility of Jesus Christ* and a novel entitled *A Stranger Among Us*. He and his wife, Ashley, are the parents of fifteen children and live on a small hobby farm outside of Charlotte, North Carolina.

IMAGE CREDITS

Cover image: Eucharist © Mariusz Szczygiel, Shutterstock.com

p. VIII Suffering Christ, 1660-70 / Murillo, Bartolome Esteban (1618-82) / Spanish / Caylus Anticuario, Madrid, Spain / Photo credit: Bridgeman Images

p. 3 Portrait of Saint Teresa of Calcutta © DeepGreen, Shutterstock.com

p. 13 Saint Paul the Apostle / Pino, Marco (c. 1520-79) / Italian / Galleria Borghese, Rome, Lazio, Italy Photo credit: Bridgeman Images

p. 14 Saint Luke (engraving) / English School, (19th century) / English / Look and Learn / Elgar Collection / Bridgeman Images

p. 18 Portrait of Cardinal Newman (1801-90) (oil on canvas) / Millais, John Everett (1829-96) / English / National Portrait Gallery, London, UK / Photo credit: Bridgeman Images

p. 20 Thomas a Kempis (1380-1471) german mystic writer, engraving / Photo credit © Tallandier / Bridgeman Images

p. 22 St. Thomas Aquinas (oil on panel) / Botticelli, Sandro (Alessandro di Mariano di Vanni Filipepi) (1444/5-1510) / Italian / Abegg Collection, Riggisberg, Switzerland / Photo credit: © Photo Josse / Bridgeman Images

p. 24 The Apostle Paul / Artist: Rembrandt (1606–1669) / Source: National Gallery of Art, Washington D.C. / Licensing: Public domain, via Wikimedia Commons

p. 30 Saint Josemaría Escrivá de Balaguer. / Source/Author: Andrés Tristán Pertíñez / Licensing: (CC BY-SA 4.0) https://creativecommons.org/licenses/by-sa/4.0/deed.en

p. 32 Claude de la Colombière / Source: http://santiebeati.it/immagini/?mode=view& album=41150&pic=41150.JPG&dispsize=Original&start=0 / Licensing: Public domain, via Wikimedia Commons

p. 34 St. Vincent de Paul (1581-1660) 1649 (oil on canvas) / Bourdon, Sebastien (1616-71) / French / St. Etienne du Mont, Paris, France / Photo credit: Bridgeman Images

p. 42 Francesco St Jerome, a work of art on copper from the early 17th-century / Source/Author: Historyportal / Licensing: (CC BY-SA 4.0) https://creative commons.org/licenses/by-sa/4.0/deed.en

p. 47 Christ Saviour, c.1570 (oil on canvas) / Titian (Tiziano Vecellio) (c.1488-1576) / Italian / State Hermitage Museum, St. Petersburg, Russia / Photo credit: Bridgeman Images

p. 62 Portrait of Saint Thérèse of the Child Jesus (or Lisieux or Sainte-Face, 1873-1897) / Photo credit: © Patrice Cartier. All rights reserved 2023 / Bridgeman Images

p. 64 Saint Teresa in glory / Painting by Bernardo Strozzi (1581-1644) 17th century–Genes Musei di Strada Nuova inv n PB 49 / Photo credit: Luisa Ricciarini / Bridgeman Images

p. 68 Saint Francis de Sales, 18th century (painting) / Pianca, Giuseppe Antonio (1703-57) / Italian / Palazzo Bianco, Genoa, Italy / Photo credit: Luisa Ricciarini / Bridgeman Images

p. 74 St. Jerome praying before a rocky grotto, 1548 (oil on panel) / Hemessen, Jan Sanders van (c.1504-66) / Dutch / Photo credit: Johnny Van Haeften Ltd., London / Bridgeman Images

RECOMMENDED READING

Abandonment to Divine Providence: How to Fulfill Your Daily Duties with God-Given Purpose

Fr. Jean-Pierre de Caussade

"Let go and let God." This popular phrase captures the essence of Father Jean-Pierre de Caussade's eighteenth-century treatise on trust, *Abandonment to Divine Providence.*

Do you doubt? Do you suffer? Are you anxious about the trials of life?

Father de Caussade offers the one sure solution to any spiritual difficulty: abandon yourself entirely to God by embracing the duties of your station in life. With wisdom and gentleness, he teaches how to practice complete submission to the will of God in every situation, whether we are beginners or seasoned travelers on the way of perfection. True abandonment, he explains, is a trusting, peaceful, and childlike surrender to the guidance of grace.

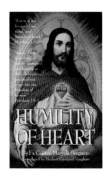

Humility of Heart

Fr. Cajetan da Bergamo

Saint Augustine said there are three virtues needed for holiness: humility, humility, humility!

Surrendering everything to Our Lord is simply not possible without the virtue of humility. Indeed, true humility naturally leads to surrender. From every direction, Father Cajetan marshals up the reasons why this virtue is paramount in the lives of all saints and of all those on the way of perfection. As no one will enter heaven who is not perfect and as no one will gain perfection who is not humble, it behooves us all to apprise ourselves of the requisites for gaining true humility of heart, for once possessing this virtue, we can then make great strides in the spiritual life. But without it, we are simply deceiving ourselves regarding our spiritual progress and postponing the great work of our own salvation.

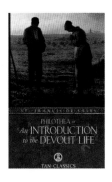

An Introduction to the Devout Life

Saint Francis de Sales

The spiritual journey, like any journey, is difficult to navigate if we do not have a good map. *An Introduction to the Devout Life* continues to lay down a path to holiness and intimacy with God that is accessible to every Christian. The beauty of this book is in its detail and simplicity.

Addressed as a personal letter to Philothea (which means "lover of God"), this book covers all the parts of a devout life:

- Our desire to lead a devout life
- Our full resolution to do so
- How we should approach God in prayer and the Sacraments
- The practice of sixteen important virtues
- Remedies against ordinary temptations
- Confirmation in our practice of devotion

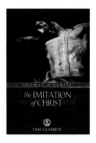

The Imitation of Christ

Thomas à Kempis

If you find yourself stuck in a spiritual rut, *The Imitation of Christ* will bring you to deeper honesty with yourself and challenge you to live a life of fidelity and moral courage.

The guide of the saints since it first appeared in 1418, it was the sole spiritual reading of Saint Thérèse of Lisieux, who loved it and knew it by heart.

Father Garrigou-Lagrange asserted that the true mysticism of which it speaks is accessible to all, if they are willing to follow the way of humility, the cross, continual prayer, and docility to the Holy Ghost.

Trustful Surrender to Divine Providence: The Secret of Peace and Happiness

St. Claude de la Colombière, Fr. Jean Baptiste Saint-Jure

To trust in God's will is the "secret of happiness and content," the one sure-fire way to attain serenity in this world and salvation in the next. *Trustful Surrender* simply and clearly answers questions that many Christians have regarding God's will, the existence of evil, and the practice of trustful surrender, such as:

- How can God will or allow evil?
- Why does God allow bad things to happen to innocent people?
- Why does God appear not to answer our prayers?
- What is trustful surrender to Divine Providence?

This enriching classic will lay to rest many doubts and fears, and open the door to peace and acceptance of God's will. TAN's pocket-sized edition helps you to carry it wherever you go, to constantly remind yourself that God is guarding you, and He does not send you any suffering too great to bear or any trial too difficult to overcome.

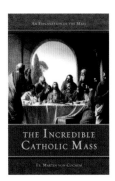

The Incredible Catholic Mass: An Explanation of the Catholic Mass

Fr. Martin von Cochem

If we are to surrender everything to God, we must go to Him in the Blessed Sacrament. Father Cochem refreshes our understanding of the reality that happens right before our eyes at every Mass. In surrendering to God's will, we must approach this most august Sacrament with humility, sorrow for sin, and awe at what God has given us in the sending of His Son, Jesus Christ, who is present now before us. Filled with true stories of miracles, this book will forever help you remain humble before Our Lord in the Blessed Sacrament.

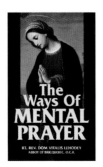

The Ways of Mental Prayer

Abbot Vitalis Lehodey, OCR

Saint Alphonsus Ligouri stated, "It is morally impossible for him who neglects meditation to live without sin." The path of surrendering everything to God must be accompanied by an ardent prayer life, including mental prayer, which is where we learn to discern God's will in our life according to our state in life and circumstances.

In *The Ways of Mental Prayer*, Abbot Lehodey concentrates on the beginning stages of prayer, up through what is called the prayer of quiet, but he also describes the higher forms of prayer as well, including the very summit, or the prayer of union. In the process, he explains the advantages, the joys, and, yes, the trials of mental prayer, plus he gives practical instructions on the methods of practicing this type of prayer.

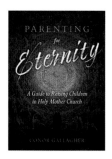

Parenting for Eternity: A Guide to Raising Children in Holy Mother Church

Conor Gallagher

Since parents are often those who feel the most "busy," this little book is a helpful tool for remembering to focus on the ultimate destination of your child.

A trillion years from now, your child will be either in heaven or in hell. And this is only the beginning of eternity. Are you really too busy to focus on where your child will spend eternity?

In light of this eternal perspective, the time is now, dear parent, to raise your child to live entirely for Christ and His Church. The time is now to train your child in the four last things, the spiritual life, the virtues of piety and humility, and the school of Calvary while shielding him from the errors of modernism, Protestantism, and much more.

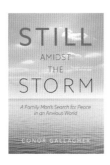

Still Amidst the Storm: A Family Man's Search for Peace in an Anxious World

Conor Gallagher

"Peace! Be still!" (Mk 4:39).

The apostles are trapped in a mighty storm, their fishing boat on the brink of capsizing ... and Jesus slept. This confused, scared, and even angered the apostles, who could not fight back the storm. But as always, Christ is our model.

In these modern times, we often find ourselves adrift in a storm of stress, anxiety, and chronic busyness. We all suffer from it. In these moments, it's easy to react like the apostles: to panic, to become angry, to be frightened.

But like Christ, we should strive to be still amidst the storm. Here, Conor Gallagher (as a father of fifteen, no stranger to life's chaos) helps you reflect upon and cultivate three remedies to the stress of modern life:

- Encountering God in the present moment, which requires a stillness of mind, to remain in the moment instead of fretting over past mistakes or future anxieties

- Listening to the voice of God, which can only be heard by blocking out the relentless noise of the world and calming our increasingly restless souls

- Resting in serene stillness by resisting the stir-crazy spirit of the world and rejecting busyness for the sake of busyness

In a world that constantly bombards us with noise, this little book offers a wealth of practical advice and real-world guidance on how to cut out stress, anxiety, and worry so that we may rest in the Lord and hear His voice, so that we may be still amidst the storm.

RECOMMENDED PRAYERS

PRAYER IN TIME OF FAILURE

By Saint Thérèse of Lisieux

Lord Jesus Christ, I have just experienced the misfortune of failing in some enterprise, and I am overwhelmed by it.

Please grant me your grace in this difficult time.

Let me realize that no one who uses all his talents ever fails in your eyes.

In addition, assist me to see that You utilize our failures to make us grow into better persons and more devoted followers of You.

Make me recall that everything good comes from You, indicating that I must work as if everything depended on me but pray as if it all depended on You.

Then if failure comes, there is a reason for it. Help me to seek and find that reason and live in accord with it.

Amen.

PRAYER FOR A BUSY LIFE

by St. Teresa of Ávila

How is it God, that you have given me this hectic busy life when I have so little time to enjoy your presence? Throughout the day people are waiting to speak with me, and even at meals I have to continue talking to people about their needs and problems. During sleep itself I am still thinking and dreaming about the multitude of concerns that surround me. I do all this not for my own sake, but for yours.

To me my present pattern of life is a torment; I only hope that for you it is truly a sacrifice of love. I know that you are constantly beside me, yet I am usually so busy that I ignore you. If you want me to remain so busy, please force me to think about and love you even in the midst of such hectic activity. If you do not want me so busy, please release me from it, showing others how they can take over my responsibilities.

AN EXERPT FROM ANOTHER
BOOK IN THIS SERIES...

You Have Only One Problem

Experience the
Instant Reward of
Trustful Surrender

CONOR GALLAGHER

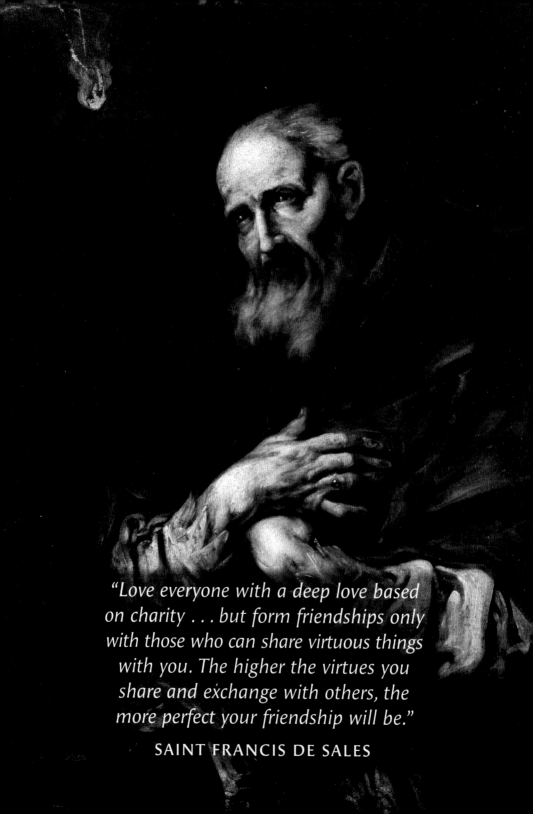

"Love everyone with a deep love based on charity . . . but form friendships only with those who can share virtuous things with you. The higher the virtues you share and exchange with others, the more perfect your friendship will be."

SAINT FRANCIS DE SALES

CONTENTS

You are ready to eliminate all your perceived problems by focusing on the one fundamental problem that all saints must face.

INTRODUCTION

What if I told you that you could remove *all* of your problems? What if I told you that you could collapse your numerous challenges into *one* problem and that you could resolve all your problems simply by dealing with this one problem?

Imagine what people would pay for a single pill that solved every medical issue from a hangnail to a brain tumor. Imagine if science could find the source of all energy, harness that energy, and apply it universally for movement and power. While those examples are not realistic at the moment, there is a path to freedom from the countless problems that give you anxiety every day.

This is not lip service, hyperbole, or exaggeration. It is real. And the saints do it every day.

If you are like most people, you have a lengthy list of problems.

- Do childhood wounds still haunt you?

- Does marriage conflict leave you exhausted and angry?

- Does financial hardship leave you worried about the future?

- Do colleagues at work irritate you to no end?

- Do adult children break your heart?

- Do you have a sick loved one with whom you would gladly switch places?

- Do you suffer continual failure due to your own shortcomings, whether it be mental, social, or physical?

- Are you confronting death in the near future?

The list could go on forever.

NO NEED FOR PRIORITIZING

If I asked you to list your many problems, big and small, it might take you all day. No doubt, you would add to the list as the day goes on. As soon as you sit in traffic, your list would grow. As soon as you have too many emails to process, your list would grow. As soon as you have to deal with an insurance company, your list would grow. As soon as you look at your full schedule, your list would grow.

When you try to diagnose your problems, when you try to grapple with them, you become overwhelmed. Often, the best advice you are given is to "prioritize them" and start chipping away at them one at a time.

While this is good advice, it fails to provide the real solution. Why? Well, if you solved your numerous problems tomorrow, aren't you going to have more problems creep back in? Isn't some irritating person, or Mother Nature, or the laws of economics going to return with a vengeance in the near future?

If you reflect on your life you will see that you have "solved" many problems. And yet, they seem to pile up faster than you can off load them.

WHY PROBLEMS PILE ON

There are a few reasons why our perceived problems seem greater than previous generations, despite the comforts and ease of modern resources:

1. **Life Complexity:** Planet earth has reached the greatest levels of complexity. As a result, you are pulled in so many directions due to technology, movement, speed, and secularism. And there seems to be no end to this uncontrollable whirlwind of complexity.

2. **Micro-vision:** In our modern times, we are used to bifurcating everything into as many little pieces as possible. This has trained your brain to see your life (especially the problems) in terms of tiny little pieces, as if your life were an instruction manual with a million pieces.

3. **Sloth:** The devil looks for ways to complicate your life. Complexity breeds sloth. Too much movement breeds sloth. Too much speed breeds sloth.

4. **Pride:** Because you are a member of a fallen race, you sometimes enjoy the drama of problems. The Irish call it the "delicious misery." Part of you, even if only a tiny part, feels important when you have many problems, and perhaps a bigger part of you desires sympathy from others. This is often called the "martyrdom complex."

The modern solutions for addressing these problems will not last. The perfect time management system will not guard you from what you experience as problems. There is no app that will make your problems disappear.

Why?

NO PROBLEMS—PLURAL

Believe it or not, you do *not* have problems—plural. Truly, you have only one problem—one problem that underlines all other perceived problems. You have one problem that springs forth from your soul and infiltrates every aspect of your life.

You are like a bird that flutters about a hundred different branches, never understanding that all the branches make up one tree.

God is watching you, right now, jump back and forth between problems. And He knows all along that there is actually one problem at the core of your soul. And if you could only climb down from all the branches, you could also see the base of this mighty tree that is your life.

"What saint has ever won his crown without first contending for it?"

Saint Jerome

Again, you do not have many problems. You do not have financial problems, or health problems, or social problems, or family problems. Do you have difficulties in these areas? Of course. Do you have tremendous suffering in these areas? Of course. But are they truly problems? In the purest sense of the word, no. These difficulties and sufferings are not necessarily meant to be overcome, conquered, defeated, or solved.

Your one and only one problem is this: you have not completely surrendered your entire being and life to Divine Providence. Once this is done (or at least begun with intent), you will begin to see all the other difficulties and sufferings as from the infinite hand of a loving Father. They are no longer "problems" but gifts—perfectly customized gifts for your salvation.

The good news is that you are not alone in this struggle. Most saints did not become saints overnight. They, too, experienced moments of uncertainty, doubt, anxiety, mental confusion, and intense suffering. Their lives were filled with more "problems" and obstacles than anyone. But with time, they came to see these problems with supernatural faith as their greatest treasures.

You Have Only One Problem

Experience the Instant Reward of Trustful Surrender

CONOR GALLAGHER

CHAPTER 2

THE ONE PROBLEM

Your one problem is that you have not trustfully surrendered every single aspect of your life to Divine Providence.

"If we could see all He sees we would unhesitatingly wish all He wishes. We would beg Him on bended knees for those afflictions we now ask Him to spare us."
Saint Claude de la Colombière

TRUSTFUL SURRENDER

The etymology of surrender has French and Latin roots. The word literally means "to give yourself back to whom you are owed." As God is your author, your creator, your source of being, it is only fitting that your end, your purpose, your final calling is to be given freely back to Him. And of all the 117 billion people who have lived on earth, you are the only one who has the power to surrender yourself back to Almighty God.

At its core, trustful surrender means seeing everything from God's perspective. Everything! We call this "surrender" because you must humbly submit your will, your hopes, your dreams, your situation, your body, your mind, your relationships, your everything to His will. Metaphorically, you wave the white flag.

"Amen I say to you, unless you be converted, and become as little children, you shall not enter into the kingdom of heaven."
Matthew 18:3

You give up the fight, that is, you stop trying to control your present and your future. And you stop regretting your past. You accept everything, good and bad, as something carefully prepared for you. And we call this form of surrender "trustful" because you

are like a child that jumps into the arms [...] a care in the world. There is no fear of [...] arms are the safest place in the universe [...] upon a child in his father's arms.

Saint Claude de la Colombière, the spi[...] Margaret Mary, posed the obvious ques[...] asking while at the same time answering [...] attribute it to God when we are unjustly [...] the only person you can charge with the wrong you suffer, He is not the cause of the sin the person commits by ill-treating you, but He is the cause of the suffering that person inflicts on you while sinning."

WHY EVERY MOMENT IS PERFECT

When you have accepted the seemingly unacceptable, when you have seen that every difficulty is an act of love for your salvation, your experience of a solitary moment is transformed. Every moment in your life—which includes this one, and this one, and this one—is perfect.

Perfect? Even those moments filled with pain? Even those moments filled with sin?

God perfectly designs every moment to give you the best chance of reaching heaven. Would a loving father ever put his child in an occasion of sin? No. A loving father constructs an environment that is conducive to virtuous living. Unfortunately, we often think you know better than God. And perhaps God allows evil over the Creator, vice over virtue. But a loving God will use this thing, even in itself to bring his child to [...] even a sorrowful moment is an incredi[...] tion and conversion!

"In the evening of this life, I shall appear before You with empty hands, for I do not ask You to count my works. All our justice is stained in Your eyes. I wish, then, to be clothed in Your own Justice and to receive from Your Love the eternal possession of Yourself. I want no other Throne, no other Crown but You, my Beloved!"
SAINT THÉRÈSE OF LISIEUX

CHAPTER 5

THE LAST 1 PERCENT

You are ready and able to take an extraordinary shortcut to total surrender by figuring out the very last thing you would surrender, passionately offloading this final perceived problem.

everything. What else can I give you?" [...] the voice of God. At hearing this, a sadn[...] man. It was all he had left. He must h[...] the many years of service not enough? [...] heart not enough? Did the Lord really d[...]

The old man wrestled with this request [...] felt heaven slipping away. He felt the Lo[...] Him. He realized that he had given 99.9 [...] Lord, but not everything. The next morn[...] to the first beggar he could find. The be[...] tempt on the gift, for he preferred mone[...] insult to the old man. And it was then he realized that he had now given everything. He was finally free from all the problems in the world. He had given up, once and for all, his final problem. He was 100 percent surrendered.

Dear Christian, what is your tin cup?

WHAT 99.9 PERCENT REALLY MEANS

You must consider a difficult truth. Giving 99.9 percent of yourself to God means you have not been willing to give God everything. It means that on some level—even if very unconsciously—you believe that God does not deserve everything, or at least that you deserve to keep something.

This is a hard truth to accept, especially since you are trying to live a holy life. You are a saint in the making. The mere fact that you are reading this book proves that you desire to surrender to your heavenly Father. On the one hand, surrender is not an all-or-nothing proposition. It is not always black or white. Our lives are filled with many gray areas. But on the other hand, the surest way to find peace and happiness is to surrender everything.